THIS IS WHAT
HAPPENS
WHEN YOU LEAVE
ME ALONE

D.T. ROBBINS

For my wife and kids

I'm so sorry

everyone "loves" this book

This book is like a near death experience except instead of having a new lease on life I want to kill myself even harder.

Barracuda Guarisco, *Really Serious Literature*

This is What Happens When You Leave Me Alone is an actual descent into madness. It's fun, it's terrible, it's wasted, it's tragic, it's real. You'll want a drink but it won't be what you ordered and the bartender is too busy for you so you'll drink your gin martini even though you hate gin because it's what you've got and isn't that what life really is anyway?

Drew Hawkins, *Micro Podcast*

D.T. Robbins is living in a dream world if he thinks people wanna read this. I want whatever the hell he's smoking. Actually, maybe not. I like having all my brain cells.

Jack Bedell, Poet Laureate, State of Louisiana 2017-2019

Listen, half of these poems aren't half bad. So that's, like, 1/4. Or 1/8. Not sure on the math. But, still, it's definitely only a fraction.

Shawn Berman, *The Daily Drunk*

I can't say these poems slap, but after reading them, I miss Borders and being left alone. Big yikes.

Mallory Smart, author of *The Only Living Girl In Chicago*

D.T *Robbins me of my time.* Fifty-four pages. Fifty-four pages I could have spent cutting my grass blade by blade with tiny nose hair scissors – which would be better time spent, undoubtedly, than reading this "book" of "poetry". Fuck poetry. Hey, are you guys down to D.T., Fuck some poetry? Dude, you owe me fifty minutes buddy. Or twenty! I don't even know. The swirling shitstorm of these pages knocked my circadian rhythm for such a loop I can't even tell what day it is. How long did I spend reading? Where am I? Who are you? What the – hey, HEY! Put me down! Put me down!

Cavin Bryce Gonzalez, founder of *Back Patio Press*

My favorite part is the poem that references me, but considering *This Is What Happens When You Leave Me Alone* is clearly written by a full-on narcissist, I find this situational irony incredibly fitting. I imagine this is also how all the wrestlers and bands and movie stars and Daves referenced in these poems(?) would feel if DMed this manuscript at 1AM like I was: elated to see their name in print.

KKUURRTT, author of *Good At Drugs*

Yeah, I read [BOOK TITLE] – well... I told D.T. I did, but really I skimmed the first three poems and then said 'Okay, I get it.' and then read something else. You'll probably do the same thing because these poems are just that forgettable. If you like them, please feel free to unfollow me. We have nothing in common.

Tex Gresham, author of *Sunflower*

What if, this book — *jams keys into beer can, shotguns it* — *This Is What Happens When You Leave Me Alone*, *looks around... rips a giant bong hit* — like, what it if had a baby with that show, *I Think You Should Leave*? You know? Mannnnnnnnnn...

Aaron Burch, founder of *Hobart* and author of *Year of the Buffalo*

Please buy this book so he'll stop fucking talking to me about it.

Alyssa Robbins, wife of D.T. Robbins

D.T. Robbins' is full of vim and vigor. And even more vigor. His first collection brings poetry down to earth where it belongs. He's still kind of a dick, though.

Bram Riddlebarger, *Gob Pile Press*

Ladies, meet your newest literary red flag. Back off, Bukowski. Hang it up, David Foster Wallace. We got a new white man with poems about pro wrestling, binge drinking, and a severe lack of coping skills. Damn, it's like a chronic masturbator wrote a cum streaked mirror onto 54 miserable pages. PRO WRITER TIP: jacking off is not a substitute for real intimacy but it's the best we can do. Fellas, are you tired of getting pussy? Throw D.T. Robbins' *This Is What Happens When You Leave Me Alone* on the shelf and enjoy the dry spell. Hope you got an ass fetish because you'll see plenty leaving your studio apartment in a hurry when they spot this little cry for help among the real books.

Dan Eastman, author of *Watertown*

I first heard D.T. Robbins read these poems to me in a Walgreens. They were bad then and they're worse now, especially the first 50. The 51st is okay. But make no mistake, you should not read this book of poems. And you should only shop at your local drugstore or CVS. If I find you in a Walgreens there will be hell to pay. If I see D.T. Robbins ever again there will be hell to pay.

Kevin Sterne, *ALL MUST GO*

Oh, cool, just what the world needs: another angsty white man making self-deprecating jokes to get attention. We get it, your life peaked during the King Kong Bundy/Hulk Hogan steel cage match.

Chris L. Terry, author of *Black Card* and *Zero Fade*

"poems"

Conehead

Sometimes I think that I'm a wine-and-charcuterie-
and-beige-suit kinda guy, and then I realize I'm a beer-
gut-slurping-whiskey-from-a-cereal-bowl-throwing-
up-a-del-beef-burrito-in-my-neighbor's-pool-at-3am-
while-their-dog-with-a-cone-around-his-head-
because-he-just-got-his-nuts-chopped-off-watches-
me-understanding-in-his-own-dog-brain-that-he's-
got-more-shit-going-for-him-than-I do-for-me kinda
guy.

Fight Club

The last time I got into a fight was in sixth grade and halfway through the fight I got scared and started crying and ran away and never stopped running and never stopped crying and I learned to do things like brush my teeth and do my taxes and get a degree and start a family and get divorced and get remarried and buy a house and get another degree and get in debt and drink too much and worry that my kids will hate me and vote Democrat and check my Twitter and delete my Twitter and redownload my Twitter and iron my clothes and dig my own grave and keep digging until I reach the earth's core and the heat from the core melts my face off and I die along the way.

You Can Write Anything and Call it a Poem

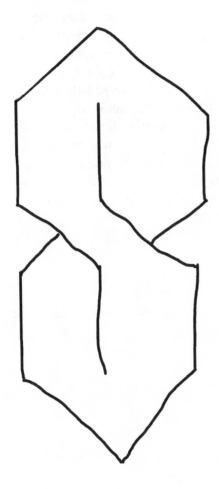

See.

Happy Halloween, Jackass

Sometimes I think I'm the papier-mâché version of a writer, melting and dripping, smelling like spit and glue, the guy that everyone talks shit about when standing next to the store-bought writer who's got like seven books published, accidentally pissing my pants and further ruining my costume, trying to explain that no no no it's not piss it's just something I spilled on myself earlier when no one was watching, filling my notebook at home with the names of everyone who made me wish I was dead, planning on running away and never coming back, moving to a commune with other papier-mâché people who all smell like me and look like me and hate themselves like me but love me just the way I am.

Then I read your poems and
HAHAHAHHAHAHAhjahahasasdHAHAAHAsaHA
HAAH!!

We both suck.

that's life, bb

The summer before I moved from Louisiana to California, before I started high school, my mom got super pissed and threw the remote control at my face and chipped my front tooth real bad.

But that's life, ya know? One minute everything is going great and the future is bright, the next you're a victim of child abuse that further perpetuates your sense of body dysmorphia and subjects you to all the insults and accusations of being a dumb fucking redneck who can't skate and doesn't know what punk is and dresses like a fucking nerd and talks like a fucking hillbilly and won't get laid and won't make friends and won't be happy and won't won't won't.

You get used to it.

Jake the Snake's King Cobra is me and I am it

A lady at work yelled at me today because something wasn't done when she wanted it done but it was her fault because she had the audacity to give a shit and make demands and strive for excellence and try.

As she's going on and on I'm thinking about Jake the Snake's king motherfucking cobra gnawing on Macho Man Randy Savage's arm. I'm thinking about how it had no fangs, no venom, no real danger, but still scared the shit outta everyone, put on a hell of a good show. I wanna go rip my own teeth out, go bald and cover myself in mud and shit, hop back on my Zoom call, smile wide and display the gaping holes all inside my mouth, blood dripping down my chin, down my chest, smear it all over the camera.

How can I help you today?

PRO WRITER TIP:

Withdraw everything, burn it in a dumpster behind Walgreens, eat raw steak, drink unicorn tears, howl at the motherfucking sun until your eyes melt into the back of your head and you finally see the world in all its bloodshot beauty.

With Arms Wide Open

when I was a freshman in high school someone asked
me to sing Creed's "With Arms Wide Open" at lunch
but I didn't because someone else said it wasn't punk

looking back, I should have fucking done it

what's more punk than shitty music paired with a voice
that's basically a shitty sorta-accent but not really an
accent and is more of a rip-off of some other asshole's
voice, going full Scott Stapp and getting blackout
drunk and not remembering the words and puking and
pissing myself and passing out in front of everyone?

also, I think the dudes who told me it wasn't punk were
into ska and so, like, fuck ska

slappity-dappity

Somewhere out in the multiverse there's a version of me who let that one time he did an impression of Adam Sandler that everyone loved and wanted to be his friend afterward go to his head, so he never stopped and ending up forever talking in the Adam Sandler slappity-dappity voice, and it made him super successful and really happy, and he ended up getting his own talk show and won a daytime Emmy and he owns the Knicks and gets recognized on the streets and went to space and his parents didn't use him against one another in the divorce and he was never homeless and is always in shape and can say no after one drink and plays golf on Sundays and is a vegan and recycles and combs his hair and doesn't live in a trashcan and hasn't had to steal water from his neighbors' hose to put in the tank of his toilet so he can flush his shit because his water got shut off and he does triathlons and loves his life and loves strangers and loves like jesus and loves loves loves loves loves loves loves.

And the Adam Sandler of that universe fucking hates him too.

Crow-Sting

after Sting went full Crow-Sting in 1996, I dealt with
my problems the same way:

parents getting divorced? Crow-Me

Heather G. said I'm 'gross'? Crow-Me

coked-out Jesus freak moves in with us, tries to kill
us? Crow-Me

mom calls the cops on dad? Crow-Me

didn't make the basketball team? Crow-Me

evicted from our house? Crow-Me

failed pre-algebra? Crow-Me

getting back acne? Crow-Me

Crow-Me, everywhere—in the corners of classrooms
and churches and courtrooms and gas stations and
summer camps and school photos and baseball games
and BBQs and family therapy and AOL chatrooms and
pool parties and Thanksgiving and campgrounds and
the mall and tucked in the back of your mind until you
finally, without question, see how sad I am.

PRO WRITER TIP II:

You can't get rejected if you give up entirely.

sup, KKUURRTT

I'm talking to KKUURRTT right now about trying to
finish this book of poems by tonight and he asked
why I wanna do that and I said idk so he said he likes
the experiment and I asked him

if I could
      use
our conversation
          to be
part of this
book
      and he said
      of course
so yeah
      now
I've got another
          poem bitches
      that's how
you fucking do

                                      it

eat shit, Walt Whitman

-poetry

giving myself pep talks before going out into the world and absolutely fucking crushing it

I keep telling myself I'm gonna stop drinking
but then I'm all bahahahahha bleeechhh pfftt guffaw
guffaw scoff scoff

I keep telling myself I'm gonna be a writer
but then I'm all bahahahahha bleeechhh pfftt guffaw
guffaw scoff scoff

I keep telling myself I'm gonna get over my
childhood
but then I'm all bahahahahha bleeechhh pfftt guffaw
guffaw scoff scoff

I keep telling myself I'm gonna make it one day
but then I'm all bahahahahha bleeechhh pfftt guffaw
guffaw scoff scoff

I keep telling myself I'm gonna find god
but then I'm all bahahahahha bleeechhh pfftt guffaw
guffaw scoff scoff

I keep telling myself I'm gonna get healthy
but then I'm all bahahahahha bleeechhh pfftt guffaw
guffaw scoff scoff

I keep telling myself I'm gonna pay off my debt
but then I'm all bahahahahha bleeechhh pfftt guffaw
guffaw scoff scoff

I keep telling myself I'm gonna make everyone proud

13

but then I'm all bahahahahha bleeechhh pfftt guffaw
guffaw scoff scoff

I'm keep telling myself I'm gonna finish this book
but then I'm all bahahahahha bleeechhh pfftt guffaw
guffaw scoff scoff

10 Dream Tag Team Pairings

Scott Hall + me completely blitzed on a Wednesday morning before work

Ted DiBiase + me turning my back on my Christian upbringing

The Undertaker + me still thinking I'm going to hell

Rick Rude + me not having sex until I was 24

Ric Flair + me at 13 yelling at my dad for not paying child support

Mr. Perfect + me gaining 20lbs after my divorce

The Ultimate Warrior + me having a panic attack at Wal-Mart

Mick Foley + me during an existential crisis

The Rock + me blackout drunk eating tacos on the floor of my apartment at 3am

Sgt. Slaughter + me during therapy

PRO WRITER TIP III:

Never stop giving up.

LIVE IT UP

one of my coworkers is super old, never married, no kids, owns a couple properties in some boujie-ass neighborhoods in Burbank, and every day when she leaves the office she tells me:

LIVE IT UP

and I wanna live it up
I really do

after work, I wanna rob a 7/11 and climb to the top of the Hollywood sign and set it on fire and call down the old gods and throw lightning from my fingertips and eat pizza with the Grim Reaper and ride a lion buck ass naked through the Hollywood Hills and buy Bitcoin and tell everyone in the whole world (except Jared Leto) that I love them and live in a bunker for a decade and come up unshaved and stinking and toothless and amazed by everything and take a shit on Jared Leto's lawn and juggle chainsaws and grow humans in the ground and find Atlantis and die and come back to life and make ice sculptures and track down Jesus Christ and ask him what the fuck bro and figure out what's wrong with me and fist fight my nightmares and learn mind control and lay out at the beach and burn my skin and feel no pain when the skin peels like Doritos off my body and go back in time and stop my cousin from dying and bench press all the pounds and delete my Twitter and redownload my Twitter and post my nudes on billboards and erase my memory and fly on a bike like in E.T. into the sun and melt into oblivion.

17

the next day I'll walk into the office and high five the shit out of my coworker and I'll keep high fiving her forever and scream that kind of scream where spit flies out of my mouth:

I LIVED IT UP
I LIVED IT UP
I LIVED IT UP
I LIVED IT UP
I LIVED IT UP
I LIVED IT UP
I LIVED IT UP
I LIVED IT UP
I LIVED IT UP
I LIVED IT UP
I LIVED IT UP
I LIVED IT UP
I LIVED IT UP
I LIVED IT UP
I LIVED IT UP
I LIVED IT UP
I LIVED IT UP
I LIVED IT UP

my name is Dave and I like to party

I used to take my empty beer cans and duct tape them
to the bottom of my new beer cans
I kinda wish I'd done that throughout my whole life

That way I could use the cans to identify the really
shitty parts of my life
and the really good parts of my life

It would make my therapist's job
way fucking easier

NDEs

I think a lot about people who've had near death experiences, how they come back and tell everyone heaven/hell is real and that they talked to Jesus or Kurt Cobain or whoever

The truth is, I'm actually kinda jealous

- a.) they feel certain about the afterlife which, I mean, cool
- b.) what a fucking ride, man

But I know that my NDE would for sure be something that would make me wanna go back and also scare the shit out of me

In my NDE I'd be a hot dog stuck on a roller at an AM/PM gas station and as the glass door opens a white light shines and blinds me and a giant pale mouth with no teeth and bloody gums would slowly reach for me and inside the mouth I hear Will Smith's "Welcome to Miami" playing from the uvula, oozing with pus, and as I go down the esophagus all these scabby hands are reaching for me and trying to grab me but I'm too greasy and I slip through and I fall and fall and keep falling in a pit of blackness and I hear my wife's voice telling me it's going to be okay and I keep calling out to her but she doesn't respond she just says it's all gonna be okay and I believe her and there's somehow peace in this and the falling doesn't seem so bad so long as I hear her voice and know that she's there even

20

if she's not there and I realize I'm not falling down a throat I'm falling more in love with her and I'm not a hot dog I'm a human heart and I'm bleeding and dying even though I'm already dead but the dying isn't so bad because she's waiting for me somewhere at the bottom and at the end of it all that's the only thing I care about.

RIP Bucky Cole whether he's dead or not

I worked at a guitar shop when I was 16 and the manager played lead guitar in a cover band

when I asked him how he prepared for a show he said, "2 Bud Lights and a joint"

best career advice I've ever received

these tweets should have gotten way more likes than they did so now I'm putting them in this book—that'll teach you not to give me the attention I desperately crave

y'all don't even like literature, quit lying

oh you hate David Lynch STFU he hates you more than you hate yourself

Del Taco > Taco Bell
FUCKING FIGHT ME!!!

Beer and creatine diet

How fucking dare everyone, honestly.

Never not normalizing nothing for nobody never in a million years, Bucko!

Made my wife listen to Korn tonight LOLOLOL PEOPLE ACTUALLY TATTOOED THIS FUCKING BAND'S NAME ON THEIR BODY HAHHAHAHAHAHHAHAHAHAHAHAHAHA HHAHAHAHAHAHAHHAHAHAHAHAHAHA HAHAHAHHAHAHAHAHAHAHAHAHHAHAHA HAHAHAHAHAHAHAHAHAHAHAHAHAHAHA HAHHAAHAHHhhahahHahahahshahahhddifwkajcn eiviwjsiwijf

Thank u god for making me way chiller than these other fucking nerds in this category

Fuck Morrissey and the punctured bicycle he rode in on.

Dreamt last night that I met an author I admire in person and the first thing they did was yell at me.

Fuck Twitter. I'm gonna find all y'all on LinkedIn and start some shit there.

It's jort season.

Hail Hydra when you orgasm.

If there's a musician I'm really in to, I'll start watching their YouTube videos, then learn how to play their songs, then find out where they buy their outfits, change my name to theirs, call their moms to tell them I love them, file their taxes, crash weddings they're invited to.

When the pizza is all gone but there's still ranch left over, I know I fucked up.

My favorite dream is that one where I steal half your pushcart awards and burn them in a giant pile like that Joker scene from The Dark Knight.

Part of me knows I should start waking up earlier, tackling my day, and being more productive and stuff. The other part of me hasn't come to hate myself that much yet, though.

I'm on a strict diet of Truly & Funyuns.

yeah no, I'm definitely "going for a thing"

My favorite part of 2021 is that I'm already kinda drunk.

I'm in the new Spider-Man movie. I play Spludder-Brung from an alternate universe. My powers consist of eating waffles, melting deodorant, pissing Shasta, and being really into ICP.

Twitter is a cry for help for all of us.

I feel attacked. No reason. Just do.

When God reads all of our Twitters, we're all going to hell.

I have no good news to share.

Cancel all literature.

PRO WRITER TIP IV:

Stop believing in yourself. No one else does.

IT was terrifying but did you ever see *Little Monsters* with Fred Savage? holy shit, man

one of these days I'm gonna unzip the flesh from my
body and walk around like Inside-Out Boy from
Nickelodeon—you know, that Claymation kid

except I'll be bloody and grotesque and amazing

everyone will freak the fuck out not because of my
ugliness but because they'd thought on the inside I
was a good guy with a good heart and a good brain
and a good soul and good teeth
the liver won't surprise anyone

I'll run up and down the sidewalks, chasing everyone,
using my intestines as a lasso to
round them up, screaming maniacally
ahahahahaahahahahaahahahahahahahahahahahhahahaha
hhahaahhahahahahahahahahahahha

the children will laugh and cheer and weep and
wowowowowowowowowowowow

people will say, don't get too close
it'll bite your face off, tear your heart out, snort your
eyeballs, swallow your lungs,
burn your esophagus, rip you right down the fucking
middle

27

there, in the sunlight, on national news, beaming
naked and lucid and present

I can finally be the monster I've always felt I was

a really good writing day of shitty writing for writers and shit

I only wrote one poem
today
but I am all hopped up
on DayQuil and Robitussin
so I'm honestly

really disappointed in myself right now

me getting healthy and y'all not being able to handle it

ALMOND FLOUR is a healthy substitute for things like regular flour, drugs, divorce, religion, gluten, smelling your own fart, bread bowls, Conor Oberst, crying at the counter in Walgreens, hyperbole, jerking off into old socks, bourbon, Jurassic Park III, cold showers, dehydration, The Smiths, flu season, getting punched in the dick, snorting paprika, KISS, burning in hell for ever and ever and ever amen, gangrene, World War III, peanut oil, GOP, lead-based paint, driving a bus through your ex's house with Welcome To The Jungle fucking ripping on the radio, poor grammar, nightmares, cyberbullying, hey man c'mon I gotta piss hand me that cup nah don't pull over I can do it just hand me that cup yeah there we go I got it oh shit there's a hole in the cup fuck man I can't stop pissing fuck dude I'm sorry man it's dripping on your seat man fuck aw man shit fuck, dairy, The Smiths, dad records all our phone calls with mom because he's still trying to get full custody, KFC, drinking gallons of candlewax, fuck man I don't wanna do this shit anymore, Christianity, Himalayan salt, Jared Leto, too many beers so you thought it'd be a good idea to take off your shoes and walk into the ocean and keep walking until the salt water burns your eyes and you don't have to worry about tasting your own tears anymore because it all tastes like tears now hallelujah, Chip and Joanna Gaines, soda, Susan Orlean's drunk tweets, too much caffeine, heartburn, canker sores, speed, the deacons of the church saying you're gonna do so much good shit for god lolololololz, nicotine, itchy asshole, Transcendental Meditation, comic book movies, white bread, scented candles, your high school girlfriend throwing a party at her friend's house and telling everyone at the school but not inviting you because you're a zit-faced piece of shit hahahahah fucking loser, dad bods, trans fat, fruit juice, The Smiths, La Croix, the finale of Hostel II where that chick cuts that dude's dick off because he called her a cunt, the incessant fear that your wife or kids are going to die because all you sorta know is loss and you'll lose it entirely and just fucking off yourself if that ever happens but don't say that shit to anyone otherwise they'll think you're nuts and pills and pills and pills and pills, starting a podcast, cholesterol, Shasta, herpes, the ice age, FILA shoes, picking up dog shit in the backyard and throwing it over the fence into the neighbors' yard because they always park in front of your house on trash day so you have to put the trash in front of the fire hydrant and the trash company doesn't pick up your trash because that's supposedly illegal or some shit even though it's probably not that trash guy is just a real POS, writing poetry, being told by your ex-wife the reason she finds you attractive is because you're so unattractive, MFAs, acid reflux, tide pods, athlete's foot, bloody noses, The Smiths, being an influencer, tooth decay, having such fucking horrible nightmares that you have to go to bed with Home Alone playing on the television because as a grown man you need to feel the sense of security you did before your whole fucking life went fuuuuccccckkkk yoooouuuuuuuu, premature ejaculation, Pilates, house music, sweeping up your grandfather's tombstone and crying and asking are you proud of me? even though you know he probably wouldn't have been so this fuels your ongoing shame in who you are as a man and a person and a human and a living thing, red meat, pizza, coffee creamer, having a heart attack at the Walgreens counter and shitting yourself in front of all these strangers and dying without hope, bacon, cereal, bottled smoothies, charred meats, fast foods, energy drinks, brown rice, breakfast biscuits, BBQ sauce, diet ice cream, sports drinks, cheesecake, margarine, meatloaf, finally letting the blackness surround you and letting the last bit of air out of your lungs and letting the earth take you and letting the fire burn you and letting the universe reclaim you and letting your loved ones mourn you and letting go letting go letting go letting go.

I cried at the end of the 1987 movie "Mannequin" when I was a kid

my mom made me watch the movie on HBO in '88 or
'89 and all I remember is bawling at the end when
Andrew McCarthy marries Kim Cattrall in the front
window of a department store as Starship's
"Nothing's Gonna Stop Us Now" plays in the
background

that's it
that's the poem, man

just imagine a four or five year old me
tears streaming down my cheeks
snot sliding into my mouth
veins popping out of my neck
writhing on the carpet
super stoked for Andrew McCarthy
for finding true love
for giving up on reality
for giving up on human touch
and fucking a plastic doll

I want everyone to be that happy

PRO WRITER TIP V:

whatever you're trying to write, someone else already
did it better

high school in Mississippi was rad if you're a little bit into masochism

during freshman year of high school a goth girl jumped out from around the corner in the cafeteria and spit in my face wet and chunky and sticky and stinking like she'd been letting the food turn to rot inside her mouth for a million years and when she did it she looked at me bug-eyed and amazed either at the fact that she'd gone through with it or the fact that I just stood there staring right back at her with a stupid grin on my face in love and heartbroken all at once

just imagine how pumped your pastor is to ask you if you beat your meat

one of the coolest things about being a pastoral intern
at a typical evangelical church in a typical suburban
neighborhood
is the weekly purity check-ins
where everyone shares how many times they
masturbated in a single day

I ain't got no crystal ball

the day I can no longer get rid of
     a Sublime song that's stuck in my head
is the day I know I'm going to die
I'm just one Santeria away
from eternal silence

the best horror movie you'll never see is everyone else watching you completely fuck up your life

stone cold drunk
sneaking into a movie theater
to see Slender Man
shouting, oh noooooo
when the first person gets killed
and causing a group of teenagers to walk out
is how I'd like to be remembered
when I die

when Fergie sang, "no, no, no, no, don't phunk with my heart" I felt that

Fergie pissing herself on stage
during a Black Eyed Peas concert

me sharting in my driver's seat
as I'm getting pulled over by the cops

same energy

Walgreens is the nexus of all human suffering and untimely demise and I love it here

every time I see a social media influencer post
something about
"being your most authentic self"
      I imagine
stripping off my clothes
going to Walgreens
stealing a bottle of white wine and a pack of Camels
swimming into a sea of traffic
      on the 210 freeway
picking a fight with God
like Lieutenant Dan in the storm
and either making peace or making funeral
arrangements

PRO WRITER TIP VI:

If your family and friends support your writing, they are enablers and are toxic.

**got blackout drunk and woke up the next morning
with this in my Notes app and have no clue what it
means but dammit if it don't make you think**

why is it called a damn word spiral
I feel like the people who really go
deep deep deep deep
deep deep deep deep
deep deep to get it go
down all the way down
(his downs) you can go and
you see something you
see something in the
middle of the fucking
mulch the fucking shit
deep deep deep deep
deep

obligatory poem about the moon

the moon is
       tight
but not as
       tight
as your mom's
       butt
shut the fuck up about the moon

babe wait babe no babe babe babe babe babe no wait babe no

I tell my wife all the time that I have to die before she
does and she says no no no babe you have to die
before me and I say no babe you don't understand if
you die before me I'm gonna

live under a bridge and do every drug all at once
which will
change my molecular structure and
give me fangs where my eyelashes were so whenever
I sob into my bowl of tater tots, I
draw blood which
attracts rabid possums that
sleep with me in my tinfoil sleeping bag
covered in rotten Miracle Whip to
keep away the ghosts of Hollywood Boulevard who
offer me cigarettes laced with
cat piss and vinegar which I
snort off the urinals in Union Station, the
cops will try to arrest me but I'll
fight them off with my
chainsaw arms and
flee to the desert where
aliens abduct me and
probe me and
conduct all kinds of
fucked up experiments but I
kinda like it because
at least I can feel something until they
drop me off at the Del Taco in Barstow because they
got sick of all the

crying and the
bleeding, so I
crawl back under my bridge and
carve your name into my chest with a
rusty knife for the hundredth time, pleading
please come home
please come home
please come home
please come home
please come home
please come home
please
please
please

my first car was a 1989 Suzuki Samurai that I wrecked three times before I turned 16

I pulled over at 1 a.m.
hissing steam
into a ghost town gas station
and gagged the radiator
on a water hose
staring at the cemetery
across the street
thinking, *this is where things go to die*

I'm home.

my very first poetry reading lolololz good job!

I'll stand in your living room with grease on my shirt
and cigarette ash in my beard

I'll read the poems from this book, halfway between
sobbing and manic laughter

I'll watch the audience, watching me, faces painted in
horror and delight

I'll put splinters under my fingernails, drink blood,
shave my eyebrows—it's all drama, baby
         the words will never be enough haha

I'll wait for applause, and wait and wait and wait and
wait and wait and wait

I'll lock myself in your bathroom, burn my clothes in
the trashcan, draw a hot bath

when the cops get there, they'll wanna know how I
broke in
sometimes I need to let myself go
big chaos energy, ya feel?

<u>Would You Rather?</u>

Savage Garden singing
truly, madly, deeply
as you're being thrown
into a woodchipper

or

living with yourself

Shia Labeouf will play me in the biopic about my life and he'll fucking nail it

Loitering in the cologne
section of Walgreens,
pouring every bottle of
Davidoff Cool Water
over my head,
screaming at the manager
about how unfairly I'm treated
on Goodreads
will be my rise to stardom.

hell in a cell

cage match
me vs. my anxiety
I go for the pin
but
the Undertaker
drags us both under the ring
straight to hell
everybody wins

once you pop

my elementary school P.E. teacher
told me that I run
like I have a potato chip
stuck up my ass

years later
I saw someone stick
a can of Pringles
up their ass

I get it now

PRO WRITER TIP VII:

Cancel yourself before Twitter does it for you.

I'd give it negative stars if I could

my professional goal is for someone on Goodreads to
compare my poems to Kevin Costner's American
accent in Robin Hood: Prince of Thieves—

"he didn't even try"

walking in a winter hellscape

secretly getting drunk
on a Zoom call
with 100+ coworkers
knowing they're all
just as miserable
as everyone else
(except that asshole in the sweater)
but no one can leave
videos must stay on
so we can all watch each other
decay and
slip further into madness
is my favorite way
to celebrate the holidays

I don't want the world to see me

if they ever do
a remake of American Psycho
I hope during the scene where
Patrick Bateman kills Paul
they replace
that Huey Lewis and the News song
with Iris by Goo Goo Dolls

you can't cancel me if it was a good joke

in 8th grade I got suspended
for pretending to jerk off
with a stick
during P.E.
I lied and said
I didn't do it
my mom went to the office
defended me
told the P.E. teacher off

twenty-five years later
this is my official confession
I'm sorry for everyone I hurt

but that shit was funny as hell lolz

Zero Cool

when someone inevitably
hacks into my email
they'll see how much time I spend
on eBay searching for
VHS copies of that movie
Hackers
about hackers who hack other hackers
and they'll be like
aw shit
this is my dude

<u>Ohhh yyyes!</u>

I'd bet anything
Paul Bearer
was a goddamn stallion
in the sack

the last one

when I get super fucking old

and my body starts dying
and my skin starts sagging
and my eyes lose their sight
and I can't hear for shit
and I can't eat solid food
and I have to piss and shit through a tube
and I smell like tapioca
and my ear hair grows to my shoulders
and my fingernails fall out
and I finally lose my mind

I will forget everything except

how to draw the Stussy symbol

about D.T. Robbins

who cares?

Constantine the Great

A Captivating Guide to the First Christian Roman Emperor and How He Ruled the Roman Empire

Contents

Introduction

Constantine the Great is a complex figure surrounded by controversies and contradictions. The sources history left for us to read are often biased one way or the other as he is the first Christian Roman emperor. His own propaganda paints a bright picture of his actions and his personality, while on the other side, we have his political enemies who paint him in much darker colors. All the sources available to us are either fully supporting Constantine or are strictly against him. There is no objective work that will give us any true insight on how Constantine lived, what he was thinking, and what his true motives were. In truth, contemporary historians served the purpose of writing what the people wanted to hear. They followed the latest political and cultural trends, and they did not care too much about objectivism and truth. Most of the historians who wrote about Constantine were Christians themselves, and they wrote in the emperor's favor not because they believed in Constantine's righteousness but for personal gain. For example, Eusebius was a Christian historian who pleased the emperor with his propaganda so much that he was given the appointment of the bishopric of Caesarea. Personal gain was a driving force for contemporary writers and historians, and even though they are our only source, we should always read their works with a grain of salt and question the motives behind each paragraph.

Another great source of the events surrounding the persona of Constantine the Great is his coinage. He issued new mints with each victory against the "barbarians," and one could say that it is in this coinage that we can observe what happened through Constantine's point of view. Coins were imprinted not just with the scenes and symbols of victory but also with inscriptions, which often tell us of Constantine's political views and actions. Even the civil wars got their own mints with inscribed general terms such as "blessed calm" or "perpetual peace," as it was a delicate thing to celebrate events in which Romans killed other Romans. Constantine's sons were depicted on coins, too, giving us a clear picture of the emperor's hopes for the future of his empire. Even the lack of Crispus's portrait after he was put to death tells us of Constantine's anger and disappointment that he must have felt toward his oldest son.

In the end, the most accurate insight on the personality of Constantine the Great we can find is from his surviving correspondence and the edicts he issued. Although he had a plethora of secretaries and advisors who helped him with the documents, we can say that the original thought and attitude behind them comes from Constantine himself. Quite a few of these documents were even written by his hand, and we can learn a lot about his political and religious views by looking at them.

All these sources we mentioned are Constantine's own propaganda. But there are several pagan writers who saw Constantine as an inadequate emperor who allowed Christianity to become the main religion of the Roman Empire, and, of course, these writers were his political enemies. In their writings, they are often very quick to harshly judge Constantine and blame Christianity for the Roman Empire's downfall. For example, Zosimus, a Greek historian from the 6th century, criticizes Constantine's religious views, which he uses to interpret the military failures of the empire.

There are also a few contemporary authors who tried their best to stay impartial and give us an objective view on the rule of Constantine the Great, but they are few. And their own impartiality is often tainted by the biased sources they were forced to use in their own writings. It is their personal experiences of the empire they lived in that stayed truly impartial, which can help fill in the gaps we have when reading Eusebius or Zosimus. The questions like what sort of a man was Constantine and what exactly did he achieve during his reign are still baffling historians. It is through tracking the right material and reading in between the lines that we can give some sort of answer. We must use our common sense to discern the truth in the pages of propaganda and paint a new, more accurate picture of Constantine the Great, his deeds, and his persona.

Chapter 1 – The Early Life of Constantine the Great

Marble bust of Constantine the Great found at the Capitoline Museums in Rome

It is not an easy task for historians to discern the true facts about Constantine the Great. He was a great man who lived during a turning point in history, as Christianity was beginning to take over the old Roman pagan pantheon. Since the writers of that time were either serving his own propaganda or composing stories that would bring about his downfall, it is very difficult to even pinpoint Constantine's exact birth year. We know the date was February 27th, but the year is somewhat obscure. Constantine was a man who always wanted to show himself as a young ruler, and through his propaganda, he claimed he took the crown at a very young age. His supporters and admirers claimed he was born either in 280 or in 282 CE. However, we know he was between 62 to 65 years old when he died in 337 CE; therefore, he must have been born around the year 272. This is also the year modern historians accept as the most accurate year of his birth.

If we look at the place of birth of Constantine the Great, once more we cannot be sure what is propaganda and what are the facts. The most likely birthplace of Constantine was Naissus in Upper Moesia, which lies in today's city of Nis in Serbia. It is unknown if Constantine proclaimed this city his birthplace since he needed solid ties to Emperor Claudius II Gothicus, who Constantine claimed was his ancestor. Or maybe he was actually born there, and the victory that Emperor Claudius won over the Goths at this site simply gave Constantine the idea of proclaiming Claudius as his ancestor. Other cities have been proposed to be the birthplace of Constantine the Great; however, Naissus remains the most likely one and is also the one most accepted by modern historians.

What we do know for certainty are some facts about Constantine's father, Constantius I Chlorus. He came from the region of Dacia Ripensis (south of the river Danube in today's Bulgaria) and was a son of a simple goat herder and freeman's daughter. Constantius I started out as a simple soldier, but he quickly advanced to the post of an officer and had a very distinguished military career. He continued to rise through the ranks to the position of praetorian prefect of Emperor Maximian and gained status as a Roman citizen, which opened up the opportunity to become a part of the Roman Empire's political life, not just the military. Contemporary writers often described Constantius as a generous and kind man, who, despite his lack of official education, was a man of culture and philosophy. Sources of Christian origin claim he was a monotheist, as one of his daughters was named Anastasia, a purely Christian name. But there is no solid evidence of his religion.

Constantine's mother was a Greek woman named Helena, who probably never married his father. She was a *stabularia*, which can be translated from Latin as a barmaid or a landlady of a tavern. She could have been the owner of a guesthouse where Constantine's father stayed during his military campaigns. There is no mention of any marriage between the two in sources, and it would be very unlikely that a Roman officer would have married a non-Roman woman. However, it was a great dishonor in those times to call someone a bastard. This is why some historians claim Constantine could not have been anything less than a legitimate son of Constantius and Helena. Although it's not known whether Helena was actually married to Constantine's father or not, it is known that she fell from his grace once he married Flavia Maximiana Theodora, the adopted daughter of Emperor Maximian. With Theodora, Constantius had six children, and it is very unlikely Constantius kept Helena as a concubine in those times. Helena, however, would rise to power once more during the reign of her son Constantine. She would appear in the art and on the coins issued by Constantine, which can only mean that she was highly respected as the emperor's mother.

As a child, Constantine spent very little time with his family. His father was always on the move as an army officer, and so, his son could not follow him to the distant lands where he campaigned. Instead, Constantine spent his youth at the court of Emperor Diocletian (244–311 CE). The Roman Empire was already practicing division under two emperors who each had his own seat of power, army, and freedom to move anywhere through the empire. This diarchy was founded by Emperor Maximian once he became Augustus (senior emperor) and appointed Diocletian as his Caesar (junior emperor) in 286. At that time, the Roman Empire was controlling the territories from Britain to Africa and from Spain to

Armenia. In fact, it was Diocletian who instituted the tetrarchy system of rule, where power was divided among four individuals who ruled separate parts of the empire. Each territory had its own capital city, while Rome was considered to be the capital of the whole empire.

One of the rulers of the tetrarchy was Constantine's father, who was appointed to the prefecture Galliae, today's Britain, France, and some territories of Germany. His capital was in Augusta Treverorum, modern-day Trier, Germany. His co-rulers were Galerius, the eastern Caesar who ruled over parts of the Balkans and Pannonia with the capital in Sirmium (nowadays Sremska Mitrovica, Serbia); Maximian, the western Augustus who ruled over "Italia et Africa" (territories of North Africa, Italy, and Spain) with the capital in Mediolanum (Milan, Italy); and finally, Diocletian, the eastern (senior) Augustus who ruled over Asia Minor with the capital in Nicomedia (Izmit, Turkey). The tetrarchy was what would eventually bring about the downfall of the Roman Empire, as it created many internal power struggles. However, at the time of Diocletian, it was a necessity as the empire was too large to defend all of its borders, especially because the Germanic tribes had started their invasions, and Dacia was already abandoned due to the constant attacks from the Goths. Diocletian was a strong ruler whose personality and politics kept the Roman Empire together, but after his death, the tetrarchy was destined to fail.

Diocletian was the senior ruler, and to ensure the loyalty of his co-rulers, he gathered their sons and cousins at his court to play the role of hostages. However, the royal hostage in these times was not treated as a prisoner or as a hostage in the modern meaning of the term. In fact, they often grew up together with the children of the emperor, enjoying the same rights and having the best education the royal court could give them. This is how Constantine spent his young age, surrounded by the best teachers of pagan and Christian origins, who taught him Roman and Greek literature and philosophy. Constantine spoke only Latin, and later in life, he would need Greek translators whenever he addressed the people. His mind and thinking were influenced by the politics of Diocletian's court, and he even accompanied the emperor on his campaign in Egypt against the usurper Domitius Domitanus, where Constantine gained insight in what it means to be a ruler of the Roman Empire. Constantine wasn't spared from court intrigues either; he was viewed as a political threat to other prominent families, and he was surrounded by jealousy and hostility from the other courtiers. As a result, Constantine had to train skills such as deception and duplicity, all the while keeping his own thoughts to himself.

Besides education, Constantine received military training, and when he came of age, he became a successful officer. First, he served as a member of Diocletian's personal guards before being transferred to Galerius's court, where he became a bodyguard. While serving under Diocletian, Constantine fought barbarians on the banks of the Danube River in 296 and fought the Persians in Syria in 297/8. While under Galerius, Constantine fought in Mesopotamia as well in the years 298 and 299. By the year 305, Constantine became a *tribunus ordinis primi* (first order tribune/officer). He returned to Nicomedia by 303, which was when the Great Persecution of Christians started.

It is no secret that Christians were often persecuted in the Roman Empire. They were an illegal religious cult, unaccepted by the citizens of the empire, and were often blamed for anything bad that happened in Rome. They were seen as members of a secret society and often characterized as evil. However, it was the anger of the people who fueled the earlier persecutions of the Christians; it was never an official state effort. Christians were often dragged out of their houses and beaten to death by angry mobs. The state rarely meddled, allowing the mobs to sate their anger on Christians more often than preventing the abuse from occurring. However, in early 302, it was Emperor Diocletian himself who asked the oracle of Apollo for advice about the Christians. Diocletian was a traditionalist, and he saw himself as a ruler who would restore the old Roman values. This included the old Roman pantheon of gods from Mount Olympus. Diocletian was a pagan to the core of his soul, and there was no room for new religions in his empire. Christians were to be persecuted as the new, unfamiliar religion, while Jews gained an exemption because their religion was old and familiar.

Initially, Diocletian thought it would be enough to remove Christians from the state's employment and military service. Galerius, however, who happened to be in the presence of Diocletian at the time, insisted that the Christians needed to be exterminated. The two rulers argued about this, and to settle the argument, they decided to ask the oracle of Apollo what would the right thing would be to do. Constantine was present at the court when the answer from the oracle arrived. The answer itself was vague, saying that Apollo could not speak due to "the just on earth." This message was enough for Diocletian, as he interpreted "the just" as the Christians, and he ordered the universal persecution and extermination of all Christians. In his later writings, Constantine said he opposed Diocletian on the matter of the Christians, and this makes it very unlikely that he took any part in the persecution. However, there is no doubt he was influenced by the events that took place. Constantine was passive during the Great Persecution, and this proved to be a political liability for him later in his life.

In 305, Diocletian chose to abdicate due to his poor health. On May 1ˢᵗ of the same year, he held a ceremony in which he declared his intentions. On the same day, Maximian in Milan had the same ceremony, as he, too, wished to abdicate. Two new Caesars were to be chosen, and everyone thought Diocletian would announce that Constantine, son of Constantius I, would be his heir. However, Galerius had influenced Diocletian heavily and made him pick his own nephew instead, Maximinus Daia. It is even believed that Galerius persuaded Diocletian to abdicate in favor of his nephew. As the Caesar of Italy and Africa, Valerius Severus was chosen instead of Maximian's own son. Severus was a close friend of Galerius, and it is obvious he influenced this election as well because Severus did not have any official training to be a leader or any relevant experience. One of the contemporary writers, Lactantius, described how the crowd that listened to Diocletian's abdication speech was disturbed to find out Constantine was not declared his heir. His description of the melodramatic surprise of the crowd is exaggerated, but it is clear that Constantine was considered as a candidate. There are also stories of hate that Galerius had for Constantine, which describe Galerius's several attempts to kill the young officer. He sometimes sent him on pointless missions in the marshes of the Danube's midsection, while in others, he would make him fight a lion alone. No matter what Galerius tried to do, Constantine would always come out victorious in these stories. But these myths are just that, and maybe there is a grain of truth about the animosity between the two. However, there is no historical evidence at all that Galerius attempted to assassinate Constantine.

With the abdication of Diocletian behind him, Constantine wanted to reunite with his father in the West. It is believed that it was his father who asked for Constantine's release from Galerius's court as he was gravely ill, but we don't know if this information is true. Other sources mention how Constantius asked for his son's help in the campaigns of Britain. What we do know is that Constantine got permission to leave the court in the East to join his father in the West. Lactantius once more gives us a very descriptive moment in his writings on how Constantine did not want to wait and risk the emperor changing his mind. Instead, he escaped the court the very same evening, and his ride was so vigorous that the horses under him died of exhaustion. Keep in mind that Lactantius was a writer of propaganda, and so, he is an unreliable source, but unfortunately, it is the only one we have concerning this matter. It is more probable that the real threat to Constantine was Severus, who became his enemy and opponent during the abdication. Nevertheless, Constantine reached his father before the summer of 305.

Constantine spent a year in Britain, fighting the Picts alongside his father beyond Hadrian's Wall. However, his father became gravely ill, or perhaps he was already ill when he called on his son to join him. Constantius I Chlorus died on July 25th, 306, in Eboracum, but not before he declared his wish that his son, Constantine, should be raised to the position of Augustus. King Crocus of the Germanic tribes, who was serving under Constantius, proclaimed Constantine the heir and new Augustus. His father's troops quickly accepted him as the new ruler and gave him their support. Gaul and Britain accepted Constantine, but Spain, which had only been under the rule of Constantius for a year, denied him.

Constantine sent a note to Galerius to notify him of his father's death and his ascension to the position of Augustus. Probably to avoid Galerius denying him the position, he was smart to accuse his father's army of "forcing" the rule upon him. This way, Constantine made sure Galerius knew it wasn't his choice to take on the mantle of leadership, but since he did, in fact, become Augustus, he had the army to back him up. It was a subtle way of saying that if Galerius attacked him, Constantine had an army who was loyal and willing to defend his position. At first, Galerius was furious at Constantine's behavior, but he couldn't just simply deny him, as it would mean an open war. Instead, he offered Constantine the title of Caesar instead of Augustus, a title that would suit the young ruler more comfortably. Constantine accepted the offer, probably to avoid the conflict himself, and was happy enough that the title made him a legitimate ruler of his father's lands. Galerius lifted his friend Valerius Severus to the position of Augustus since he was his favorite.

The Rhine River was the border of Constantius's domain, and it was an important strategic area of the Roman Empire against the Germanic tribes. The army stationed there was huge, and it was Constantine who had the power of commanding it. However, he knew he was not strong enough to take on Galerius at this point. He chose to remain steady and rule his share of the empire, which consisted of Britain, Gaul, and Spain. He stationed himself in Britain, where he could continue fighting the Picts, and he improved the roads and finished building military bases, the latter being a project his father started.

Back in Rome, the atmosphere was becoming more intense, as Maxentius, the son of Maximian, was jealous of Constantine's elevation to the position of Caesar, and he wanted the same for himself. He had no love for Galerius and was brewing a rebellion.

Chapter 2 – Early Rule

After the campaigns in Britain, Constantine finally moved to his capital in Augusta Treverorum. When the Franks learned of Constantine's ascension, they decided to invade Gaul in the winter of 306/7. This was a great opportunity for Constantine to win his first major battle as a new ruler, and he managed to drive the Franks back across the Rhine River. He even managed to capture two of their leaders, King Ascaric and King Merogais, who both died in the amphitheater of the capital Augusta Treverorum after being fed to the beasts during the victory celebration ceremony.

With the immediate threat over, Constantine launched a major expansion of his capital. He strengthened the city walls by building towers and fortified gates. In the northeastern part of the city, Constantine started the construction of his own royal palace. The audience hall of the palace was massive, and so was the imperial bathhouse. However, Constantine did not limit his building plans just to his capital. He sponsored various construction projects throughout Gaul, especially in Augustodunum and Arelate, today's Autun and Arles in France.

The persecution of Christians was still going on when Constantine became a Caesar. Diocletian had abdicated, leaving the persecution to Galerius, even though he thought the job was done since the Christians were eliminated from military and state positions. It was

Galerius who understood that it would take a much bigger effort to permanently get rid of elusive Christians. In the end, the persecution was unsuccessful, as the Christians found various ways to defy the Roman Empire. Some bribed the state officials to stay in their position, some simply left the empire, and others hid in the woods and groves where they were safe from being targeted. Christians continued existing through the persecution, though they had to keep a low profile and stay silent as their properties were confiscated and churches were burnt. At this time, Constantine wasn't a Christian yet; however, he chose a softer policy toward them. He ended the persecution officially in his share of the empire and returned all the properties the Christians had lost during the pogrom. He even allowed Christians who were running from the "Great Persecutor" Galerius to settle in the lands he ruled.

Maxentius's Rebellion

As it was the custom, Constantine's portrait was brought to Rome upon his succession to the throne. There, a jealous Maxentius mocked the portrait, calling the new Caesar the "son of a harlot" while complaining about how powerless he was. Maxentius decided to seize the title of emperor in 306, thinking he deserved it even more than Constantine. However, Galerius refused to recognize him, and he even sent Severus to discipline Maxentius. But Severus was in command of the armies who were previously loyal to Maximian, the father of Maxentius. So, instead of obeying their new commander, the army decided to imprison him. To support his son, Maximian quit his retirement and took the role of emperor again. He openly asked Constantine to support his son, and in return for doing so, he would allow him to marry his daughter Flavia Maxima Fausta and grant him the title of Augustus. Constantine agreed, but he was reluctant to join the fight openly. He admitted Maxentius as being the emperor in Italy, but other than political recognition, Constantine did not offer any other kind of help.

In order to avoid a direct role in the Italian conflict, Constantine returned to Britain under the excuse of Pictish incursions. He sent his army to fight the Germanic tribes along the Rhine to avoid sending them as military aid to Maxentius. Because he avoided direct conflict with the rest of the empire, Constantine became very popular among the common people. Instead of paying attention to the internal state conflicts, he toured the country, investing in the arts and economy and becoming even more popular. Maximian stayed with Constantine for a year, but upon his return to Rome, he had a fallout with his son. Many believe that their argument was staged in order to trap and dispose of Severus, but there is no historical evidence to support this view. However, soon after the death of Valerius Severus in 307, Maximian and Maxentius reconciled, and Maximian once more took the title of Augustus and shared the rule with his son.

On November 11th, 308, Galerius called all the rulers to a general council. He deliberately did not invite Maxentius because he influenced his father Maximian to resign once more. He now needed a second Augustus to rule the West while he ruled the East, and he chose Gaius Valerius Licinianus Licinius, his comrade-in-arms, who had never even served as Caesar. This decision angered his nephew Maximinus Daia, who retained his title of Caesar instead of receiving a promotion while this newcomer Licinius was elevated to the role of Augustus. Maximinus demanded a promotion from Galerius, who, in turn, offered him the title of "son of the Augustus" (*Filius Augustorum*). The same title was offered to Constantine, who was now demoted back to Caesar since his promotion by Maximian was considered to be illegitimate. However, neither Constantine nor Maximinus accepted this new title, and Galerius had no other choice but to refer to both of them as Augusti by the end of spring in 310. With Constantine being the new Augustus in the West, Licinius was left with the control of only the Illyrian provinces.

Maximian's Rebellion

In 310, Maximian, even though he had abdicated from the position of Augustus for the second time, remained restless, and he tried to raise a rebellion against Constantine at whose court he retired. Constantine sent him, along with a contingent of troops, to Arles, fearing that Maxentius would attack southern Gaul. Once there, Maximian proclaimed Constantine dead and took the royal purple for himself. However, the army remained loyal to their legitimate emperor, and they forced Maximian to leave the city. To gain some followers, he offered large amounts of money to anyone who would support him. Still, it wasn't enough, and the people showed their love for Constantine to be greater than that of gold.

Once Constantine heard of the rebellion, he abandoned his campaign against the Franks and started the march up the Rhine. Maximian's only choice was to flee and seek refuge in Massilia (Marseille, France), a town that could withstand long sieges. However, Maximian did not count on the citizens' loyalty to Constantine. As soon as he approached the city, the people opened the back gate to their emperor and his army. Maximian was quickly arrested and reprimanded for his crimes against the only emperor who was willing to take him in after his second abdication. Constantine obviously respected Maximian, probably because of the friendship Maximian showed to his father, but he could not forgive this betrayal. Instead of dealing out severe punishment, Constantine encouraged the ex-Augustus to take his own life. Maximian hanged himself in July 310.

There is some controversy behind the death of Maximian, as the sources claim it was Constantine who said his suicide was a family tragedy. However, a year after Maximian's death, Constantine offered another story. Instead, he claimed that he granted a pardon to Maximian after his rebellion and offered him to stay with him and his daughter Fausta at the royal court. But Maximian plotted to kill Constantine, and due to the loyalty of his wife, he survived. In fact, when Constantine learned about the plot, he ordered a eunuch to sleep in his quarters the night of the planned killing. Maximian was arrested while performing the deed, but Constantine was still merciful enough to offer him the choice of suicide rather than to disgrace him with public execution. This second story might have been a fabrication and the propaganda of Constantine himself, who issued a *damnatio memoriae* (condemnation of memory) on Maximian.

Constantine ordered the destruction of everything that referred to Maximian in any way, be it by name or picture.

However, Maximian offered support to Constantine in the past, and he was the source of his legitimacy as an Augustus. Now that the old emperor was dead, Constantine needed a new source of that legitimacy if he wanted to keep his respectable public image. After Maximian died, he fabricated a dynastic connection to Claudius II, a Roman emperor from the 3rd century. He even gave a speech to make this fact publicly known. Claudius II (214–270) was famous for defeating the Goths near Naissus in Upper Moesia, where Constantine was born. Claudius was also known for restoring order throughout the Roman Empire. Because he claimed family connections to this emperor, Constantine also claimed the ancestral prerogative to rule alone. He was obviously dismissing the idea of the tetrarchy, realizing its instability after the unrest that followed Diocletian's abdication. To support his claim that the empire needed a sole ruler, Constantine said he experienced a divine vision sent by Apollo, who Constantine was a devoted follower of. In this vision, the god himself granted Constantine laurel wreaths, a symbol with which he blessed the Augustus with health and long rule. At the same time, Constantine issued new coins that replaced Mars as his patron deity with Apollo, the sun god. Of course, his proclamation of dynastic ties with Claudius II and of this divine vision is nothing more than propaganda; however, it should be noted that it did make an impression on his followers. He became especially popular among the citizens of Gaul after these proclamations.

Hearing of his father's death, Maxentius presented himself as a devoted son. He swore he would avenge his death and started issuing coins with the image of his disgraced father, probably to inspire the people's support.

Chapter 3 – Civil Wars

A fresco depicting the battle between Constantine and Maxentius
(Source:https://en.wikipedia.org/wiki/Constantine_the_Great#/media/File:Battle_of
_Constantine_and_Maxentius (detail-of-fresco-in-Vatican-Stanze)
c1650_by_Lazzaro_Baldi_after_Giulio_Romano_at_the_University_of_Edinburgh.
jpg)

By the mid-310s, Galerius was ill and unable to make any good
political decisions. His last act was a proclamation of the end to the

persecutions of Christians and the return of the Roman Empire to religious tolerance. He died in April or May 311, soon after the proclamation was issued. His death was due to a horrible, gruesome illness, possibly gangrene or bowel cancer. With his death, the tetrarchy ended. Maximinus moved quickly against Licinius, who had just lost a friend and supporter. Following Constantine's example, Licinius fabricated his dynastic ties to another old Roman emperor in order to set himself as the sole ruler after the death of Galerius. He claimed he was the descendant of Philip the Arab (204-249), which fortified his position. Maximinus managed to take over Asia Minor through peaceful solutions as Licinius agreed to share the eastern provinces between the two of them.

At the time of Galerius's death, Constantine was touring Britain and Gaul, while Maxentius prepared for war to avenge his father's death. He hoped to gain Christian support by allowing them to elect a new bishop of Rome. Even though Licinius also claimed the right of sole rule over the Roman Empire, Constantine regarded Maxentius as the bigger threat and decided to move against him. In fact, he made an alliance with Licinius in the winter of 311 when he offered him his half-sister, Flavia Julia Constantina, as a wife. However, by making this alliance, Constantine made an enemy of Maximinus, who kept trying to wrestle power from Licinius. In response to this alliance, Maximinus sent ambassadors to Rome, offering political recognition to Maxentius if he would give him his army in return. Maxentius agreed and began preparations for war. It is noteworthy that contemporary writers describe how it was impossible to travel between regions at those times and how everyone expected the political tensions to culminate into a war at any moment.

By the early spring of 312, Constantine gathered his army, but he decided to move only a quarter of his forces against Maxentius. His generals, advisors, and even soothsayers advised him against the preemptive strike, but Constantine ignored all of them. Many people believed he was driven by some divine power, and they were eager to follow him. Constantine took around 40,000 men on a march to cross the Cottian Alps and attack Maxentius. The first town Constantine encountered in Italy was Segusium (Susa), and he took it without many casualties. The town did defy him, but he ordered the gates to be burned down and the walls scaled. After a quick, decisive victory, Constantine forbade the looting and pillaging of the city, and he then marched his army farther into northern Italy.

It was at the gates of Augusta Taurinorum (Turin) where Constantine encountered the first heavily armed cavalry of Maxentius's army. At the Battle of Turin, Constantine encircled Maxentius's cavalry with his own. Constantine's soldiers were equipped with iron-tipped clubs, which they used to dismount their enemies before easily defeating them. The city of Turin recognized the victory of Constantine and thus refused to open the gates to the retreating army of Maxentius. Following this victory, other cities in northern Italy sent envoys to Constantine, congratulating him on his victory. When Constantine approached Milan, the city gates were already open in anticipation of his arrival.

The next cities Constantine conquered were Brescia and Verona. While Brescia posed no challenge, Verona hosted a large part of Maxentius's army. Ruricius Pompeianus, the general of the Veronese forces and Maxentius's praetorian prefect, tried to defend the city, demonstrating his loyalty to the late Maximian. Verona was in an excellent defensive position as it was surrounded by the river Adige from three sides. But Constantine managed to cross the river on the northern side of the city and lay siege to it. In the short battle that followed, Ruricius was killed, and Verona opened its gates willingly. With the surrender of Verona, other cities soon followed, including Aquileia, Mutina (Modena), and Ravenna, opening the road to Rome, where Maxentius waited.

Maxentius prepared the city for a long siege, as he had grains from Africa and the control of the praetorian guard, who protected the impregnable walls. He also destroyed all the bridges that connected the city with the other bank of the river Tiber. This move left the rest of central Italy undefended, but Maxentius claimed it was the will of the gods. Seeing how they were abandoned, the people of that region offered their support to Constantine. Even the citizens of Rome showed hatred for Maxentius, openly taunting him by saying how Constantine was invincible. Now Maxentius wasn't sure if he would be victorious after the siege, and so, he built a wooden bridge over the Tiber that would grant him a route for his army to an open field battle if the need arose. On the sixth anniversary of his reign in 312, Maxentius asked the oracles for guidance. They prophesied that the enemy of the Roman people would die in the battle. Encouraged by these words, and not even considering that the enemy of the people might actually be him, Maxentius rode out of the city with his army to meet Constantine on the battlefield.

The battle between the two rulers of the Roman Empire was brief, and Constantine was victorious. In his attempt to cross the wooden bridge back to Rome, Maxentius fell in and drowned. His army dispersed, pushed by Constantine's cavalry, and they, too, tried to cross the Tiber River, retreating to the city. Constantine entered Rome on October 29th, 312, and the people cheered. He ordered Maxentius's body to be fished out of the Tiber and be decapitated, and his head was paraded through the streets of Rome for everyone to see. Even though Constantine launched the propaganda campaign against Maxentius depicting him as an evil tyrant and himself as a liberator, Constantine did not seek revenge on the supporters of the late ruler. The grateful Roman Senate decreed him "title of the first name," which meant that all official documents would bear his name first. They also declared him as the "Greatest Augustus," which meant he was now superior to both Licinius and Maximinus. To present himself as a benevolent ruler, Constantine issued decrees in which he returned all the properties confiscated by Maxentius, as well as recalling the citizens that were sent to live in exile and freeing his enemies from the dungeons. It appeared that Constantine liberated Rome from the yoke of a tyrant, and the people celebrated their new freedom, thus making their new emperor very popular throughout the empire.

Constantine was now very close to becoming the sole ruler of the Roman Empire, especially because Licinius and Maximinus had to settle a quarrel of their own. In 313, Constantine met Licinius, and they agreed on the Edict of Milan, which granted freedom of religion throughout the empire. Christianity was now finally legalized. However, Maximinus took the opportunity of Licinius's absence and invaded his European territories. Constantine did not offer any military help, but Licinius managed to defeat Maximinus on his own and gain full control over the eastern part of the empire. For a time, the two emperors ruled together, with Constantine in the West and Licinius in the East. However, their relationship started to deteriorate rapidly.

In 320, Constantine accused Licinius of breaking the Edict of Milan by renewing the oppression of Christians. He claimed Licinius started confiscating Christian possessions and eliminating any Christian office-holders. However, there are no unbiased sources that confirm this new oppression of Christians. It is only known that Licinius saw the Church as a tool that Constantine often used to promote his politics, but there is no evidence that Licinius openly defied Christianity in general. Nevertheless, a civil war broke out in 324 based on Constantine's accusations. Licinius was aided by Gothic mercenaries, which was depicted as an evil, old pagan force in the history of Christianity. Constantine, on the other hand, with the army of Franks behind him, was depicted as a liberator who fought under the symbol of Christ. Even though the battle between the two emperors was a battle for political supremacy, everyone saw it in religious terms. Constantine's army was outnumbered, but, inspired by the divine, they managed to gain a victory in the Battle of Adrianople (Thrace). It is said that the symbol of labarum (a symbol of Christ) was like a talisman for Constantine's army. Constantine displayed the symbol throughout the battle to motivate his soldiers, who, in turn, fought vigorously, ensuring a victory.

After his defeat, Licinius retreated to Byzantium, but Constantine marched after him. However, the narrow waters that divided Thrace from Asia Minor posed a challenge. It was Constantine's son Crispus who won a naval battle there and opened the path for his father's army. Constantine met Licinius in the final battle at Chrysopolis, which took place on September 18th, 324. Constantine launched a single massive frontal assault on Licinius's army, forgetting about any maneuvering tactics. The result was a decisive victory in which 30,000 soldiers led by Licinius lost their lives. Licinius himself managed to escape, however, and gather another force at the city of Nicomedia. But he was aware he had no chance against Constantine's growing army, and he finally gave up the fight, throwing himself at the mercy of the victor.

Initially, Constantine spared his life, probably at the request of his sister, who he had given to Licinius in marriage. However, a few months later, the army accused Licinius of planning treason and demanded his execution. Constantine had no other choice because the support of the army was too important to lose. In addition, a year later, Constantine also executed his own nephew, the son of Licinius, under the same suspicion of treason. At last, Constantine had become the sole emperor of a vast and mighty empire.

Chapter 4 – Constantine, the Lavish Administrator

Constantine was an autocratic emperor like many other Roman rulers that came before him. However, he was more open about that fact, as he would later describe his empire as a dominate, or dominion. It had become a custom to address Emperor Domitian (51–96) with the title of "domine," which means lord; however, a similar title "dominus" would only be formally adopted in the times of Diocletian (r. 284–305).

Diocletian was different from his predecessors, who preferred the simple, traditional Roman manners, as he introduced several complex rituals and protocols at his court. They were inspired by the lavish oriental customs in Persia, and Diocletian liked the luxurious silk robes with encrusted gems and complex ceremonies. He also changed the official court greeting from the polite "salutatio" salute to "adoratio," which was somewhat demeaning to those who greeted him.

Constantine's father didn't care much about formal court proceedings and sophisticated manners. He was a pragmatic man. On the other hand, Constantine himself didn't share his father's opinions on the subject. He preferred to wear lavish robes, decorated bracelets, and a great deal of jewelry. Constantine also chose to have long hair to resemble Alexander the Great, even though some of that hair was fake. His rule was transformed from the traditional role to a more sacred and divine one, inspired by the idea of Christianity's heavenly court. He took this development further, referring to his palace as the "domus divina" (temple) and introducing the word "sacrum," meaning sacred, in many of the court ceremonies.

These changes were to become even more drastic over the years. Constantine stamped new coins with his figure wearing a diadem made of pearls to signify his position as being superior to that of mere mortals. The image of the divine was intertwined with the image of the emperor. Everything from his formal garbs to his palaces, from court manners to newly minted coins, reinforced this image. Constantine sought to not only imitate Diocletian but to also exceed him by openly taking advantage of this autocratic power.

The administration of the empire also suffered a set of changes. It all started with Diocletian, however, as he had reorganized the administration by separating the military tasks from the civil tasks. Constantine continued the process by fully separating the military and civilian leadership. Under his rule, the governors of the Roman provinces lost their military commands. Instead, military duties were given to separate generals. This way, civil administration and military administration in each province would be completely unrelated. The reason for these changes was to further limit the power of the provincial governors, who had a history of occasionally raising rebellions against the emperor. Constantine gained more power over the provinces by doing this, and he also continued the centralization campaign by breaking the provinces apart into smaller administrative territories that would become easier to control. The centralization of the empire was performed gradually so that Constantine could maintain a tight grip over his dominion.

In addition to the significant administrative changes, Constantine removed the traditional aristocracy that governed under the emperor. Instead, he created the Order of the Imperial Companions, an office that would consist of people Constantine trusted and deemed as friends. Their allegiance was sworn to himself personally and not to the state. This act is important, as it represents the building block of vassalage that would later be instituted throughout Europe in the medieval period.

Constantine created many such organizations and offices in order to promote the many people he deemed deserving and loyal. Each man who received such honors from the emperor was essentially showered with wealth and status. These changes assured Constantine's control of the empire; however, bureaucracy became a nightmare. With so many institutions, the administration slowed down in performing its tasks, while costs increased significantly. The cost of the military had also increased greatly, and due to the many expeditions and campaigns the Roman legions were involved in, Constantine had to support a monstrous machine that was constantly hungry for funding and supplies. Taxes had been high since the era of Diocletian, and these new changes meant even more taxes for the common people.

In addition, Constantine led a very lavish lifestyle with his newly appointed administrators and companions. He liked to organize rich ceremonies and spend money on complex building projects. Constantine wanted to gain the adoration of the people, and in order to do so, he had to spend far more than the previous emperors. Many writers of the time seemed to agree on this aspect of spending. They write that Constantine was spending money at far higher rates than anyone since Alexander the Great's famous campaigns. They mentioned that in addition to all his projects and personal spending, Constantine was also giving the lowly citizens of the empire food and clothing, such as beggars and widows. The people adored him for doing this; however, this caused a massive increase in the number of people who did not contribute to society.

So, as one can gather, the empire needed more money, meaning taxation had to be increased. Other emperors were concerned about raising taxes too greatly because such measures were seen as oppressive to the population. Constantine, however, kept the high taxation that was instituted by Diocletian and added several other taxes of his own. He didn't just tax the poor, as he also added new taxes for the wealthy senators as well. Constantine also declared that whoever wouldn't pay his taxes on time would have to pay five times the sum. If they still would fail to deliver, capital punishment would be used. These taxes were such a high burden on society that many historians of the period wrote about its effect on the people. They noted that Constantine started making examples of those who didn't pay by torturing them in the public square. Some historians even mention a massive increase in slavery because the poor people who couldn't afford the taxes had to sell their children as slaves in order to avoid punishment.

The high taxation caused a chain reaction throughout the empire. The middle class had to contribute a great deal as well; therefore, they increased the rent for the use of their land and rural properties. The peasants became so poor as a result that many communities were abandoned as people were forced to flee. With such poor rural areas, agriculture suffered. Constantine sought to fix the problem by eliminating the punishments of torture and simply imprisoning those who could not pay. He also reduced one of the taxes, but that made a marginal difference that didn't matter on the grand scale. In time, towns and municipalities began suffering as well because much of the taxation did not benefit the people. The money went to the government, with much of it being distributed to Constantine himself in order to support his lifestyle. In addition, by 320, many luxurious churches were being constructed with those taxes as well. As a result, the middle class soon began to collapse, and the taxes became too much to bear even for the merchants and tradesmen.

The tax policies instituted by Constantine led to the downfall of all trade and agriculture throughout the empire. The increasing poverty among the classes led to increased hostilities toward the government. Inflation started impacting the economy even more, and eventually, by the end of the century, gold and silver coins would become difficult to come by. The empire became poorer, and without a doubt, this entire chain reaction would help lead to the fall of the Western Roman Empire.

As the empire went through economic struggles, corruption reached new heights. Wages shrank drastically due to the growing inflation; therefore, many public servants started accepting bribes whenever they had an opportunity. This problem expanded to the military as well, as officers started stealing from the soldiers' wages or treated them badly until they would pay a small fee. The churches accepted bribes as well from those who wished to secure a position as a priest or climb the hierarchical ladder.

Constantine was aware of the troubles of the empire. He even knew about the corruption that took place, and he wasn't pleased at all. He knew it couldn't continue unanswered because it reduced his own power over his subjects; therefore, he implemented several new laws. Penalties against acts of corruption were increased, and Constantine decreed that if anyone suspected a high-ranking official of any misconduct, that person should come forward and personally address him. The emperor became a judge as well, hoping to root out the corrupt governors and officers.

Constantine's new laws were meant to enact vengeance upon criminals and inspire order through the fear of punishment. He instructed his judiciaries to severely punish anyone who broke the law. This included punishment by death or mutilation, and it wasn't meant just for those in positions of power. Scribes who falsified papers, workers who failed to deliver according to their contract, dishonest tax collectors, and basically any member of society could be savagely punished for breaking any law. An even more extreme form of punishment, however, was reserved for crimes related to chastity. Slaves who had sexual relations with a free woman would be executed at once. Maids who would help someone kidnap her master or mistress would be executed by pouring molten lead down her throat. These are but a few examples of the brutal punishments that were designed to maintain control over a dire situation.

None of Constantine's measures had any effect. Corruption ruled, and no law would persuade the criminals and the desperate to refuse bribes and conduct themselves in a more respectable way. Even the fear of death failed to convince the impoverished population from performing illegal actions. Many historians from the time of Constantine wrote that everything (and everyone) could be bought and that death did not even slow down the corruption

Chapter 5 – The Man behind the Emperor

Behind the autocratic emperor lies a man that is difficult to truly know and understand. In order to learn who he was as a person, we need to rummage through a great deal of the flattering propaganda of the time. For instance, there were many Christian writers who admired Constantine and wrote that he was kind, charming, and loved by all. Other writers mention that everything he did was of high nobility. All of this is the exaggeration of the time, so we truly need to sift through a lot of material in order to gain real insight into Constantine's personality.

Constantine was, after all, just a man, and like any other, he was both brilliant in certain ways as well as flawed. For instance, we know that he was indeed a great general, a talented leader, and a calculated planner and organizer. He was clever, and he knew when to wait and when to strike to his advantage. However, the most valuable aspects of his character can be seen in his policies over religion, Christianity in particular.

Constantine learned a great deal at the court of Diocletian, and it is there that he studied the art of patience. He learned how to pursue a goal with care and tact, and he mastered the art of dissimulation. This would become valuable, as he would become an adherent to Christianity in order to unify the empire. He believed that embracing the Christian faith, together with the statesmen beneath him, would gradually push the entire population to do the same and become unified under one faith. His patience and gradual approach to his plan for unification can be considered the most important of his talents.

Another interesting aspect of Constantine's personality is the fact that he enjoyed conversation with the common soldier, thus inspiring loyalty into his military. As a military man himself, he delighted in discussing the familiar with his troops.

Constantine was also heavily focused on education to better himself intellectually, especially because his education was initially lacking. According to his contemporaries, he wasn't the best when it came to abstract thinking and logical arguments. However, he promoted all intellectuals and fought against any current that went against them. Constantine also encouraged education by eliminating certain taxes for those who pursued a career in the sciences and arts.

Unfortunately, this is where the real positive aspects of the emperor end. We already discussed many of his failed plans and actions, and one can see that, ultimately, Constantine was an ambitious emperor. He was emotional instead of logical, and he was even superstitious, as evidenced by his devotion to his own religious views. Nonetheless, he was autocratic about achieving his own success no matter the cost. That is one of the reasons why he implemented such ruthless punishments that, in the end, did not help to stem the tide of corruption at all. Even though Constantine strived to be patient and implement his plans gradually, he was also known for his outbursts of impatience, although they only occurred on occasion. His eagerness to achieve his goals the way he imagined them led to despotic decisions, and it did not help that Constantine did not have the ability to judge people and see who they truly were.

Constantine's character was divided into two distinct personalities. On the one side, he was patient, tolerant, and understanding, but on the other side, he could simply snap and become impatient, brutal, and vengeful. His biggest fault, however, was the fact that he was incredibly vain. Constantine enjoyed flattery, and he adored being popular. That is why he organized many ceremonies and social events, and he also tried to buy the love of the poor by giving money to the widows and beggars during his early reign. This made him easy to deceive and manipulate if enough flattery was applied. Constantine's vanity and desire to be loved pushed him to create many unnecessary offices and political organizations that drained the empire's coffers without providing anything other than social status and wealth to his friends. His generosity, in combination with his vanity, led to the economic downfall of the empire.

Toward the end of his reign, Constantine would worsen, as his positive traits were lessened and overcome by the negative ones. He started having dreams that he saw as visions, and he was often overtaken by jealousy and rage. He would also often experience bursts of fury that would lead him to murder some of his entourage due to his unfounded suspicions. For instance, Constantine executed Sopater, a pagan philosopher who was one of Constantine's advisors, in 331. Constantine blamed him for magically controlling the wind and thus causing a famine to erupt, which was due to the failed delivery of food and supplies. Many more of his friends and advisors would die the same way, as Constantine saw himself as a supreme autocrat who had the right to decide over anyone's life.

According to Eutropius and Gibbon, Constantine would continue to deteriorate greatly, and by the end of his reign, his power would corrupt him absolutely.

Chapter 6 – Constantinople

Coins minted to commemorate the founding of Constantinople
(Source:https://upload.wikimedia.org/wikipedia/commons/e/e6/Constantinopolis
_coin.jpg)

Constantine is famous for two things. He converted the Roman Empire to Christianity, and he built Constantinople, a city that would, shortly after, become the heart and capital of the Eastern Roman Empire, which is also referred to as the Byzantine Empire.

The city of Rome was still beloved at the time, and it was an important center for trade and administration; however, it had lost its reputation as the political heart of the empire. Rome was simply too far away from the borders of the empire and the numerous roads that stretched throughout the Roman territories. In addition, several military-driven emperors wanted to be away from the Senate and its influence so that they could pursue their goals without interference from state politics. These emperors developed new military and administrative centers, such as Sirmium in the Danubian provinces, Antioch in Syria, Thessalonica in Greece, and today's Milan. Over time, these cities took away from the power of Rome.

Constantine, on the other hand, was on the lookout for a new site to build a capital greater than Rome. He was searching for a location where the European road intersected the Euphrates River, through the Bosporus passage that connected the Black Sea to the Aegean Sea, and he found it. This new site was also where Constantine defeated Licinius in 324 in the Battle of Chrysopolis. There was a long tradition of emperors and successful military commanders founding a city at the location of one of their famous victories. This site was Constantine's famous victory, and in addition to that, the location was of strategic importance due to the trade routes and defensive potential it had, as the new city could be defended both by a navy and a military force.

The founding of Constantinople is assumed to have taken place around the year 326, but its actual dedication ceremony was arranged in 330. Constantine was present during the massive construction project, pushing everyone involved to progress faster and harder. In addition, he also employed the Visigoths to rise to the defense of the city as a result of a peace treaty he signed with them.

Constantinople quickly developed, as it was connected to Europe as well as the economic centers of Syria and Asia Minor. In addition, the city had access to Egypt's trade route and thus took advantage of the grain exports that also fed the city of Rome and the entirety of North Africa. As a result, immigrants flocked to the opportunities presented in Constantinople, and they were encouraged to further develop the new capital. Constantine offered land to new settlers and even gave them several tax breaks in order to boost the local economy and to further develop trade and industry. However, the massive construction projects and the large number of craftsmen required proved to be a punishing expense to the emperor. Constantine focused on multiple projects at one time, and he invested heavily in bringing statues from all corners of the empire, as well as libraries filled with both Greek and Roman works. The city developed, but it would not reach Rome's size for quite some time. When Constantine died, it is estimated that Constantinople had a population of roughly 50,000 citizens.

Constantine demonstrated prudence in his new construction project. It was clear that he wanted the city to eventually become the capital of the empire; however, at the time, he did not dare to take anything from Rome. The new city, in fact, rivaled the other important urban centers in the empire, and soon Constantine would build many lavish palaces and monuments that would make the city shine above the rest. The founding of Constantinople is significant because it would essentially move the Roman Empire to the East, as it was far richer than the old Western Empire and Italy itself.

Chapter 7 – Constantine and Christianity

A drawing on vellum depicting Constantine and the Council of Nicaea burning Arian books

During Constantine's childhood, monotheism was already progressing in society, and more and more people were joining the movement to abandon the belief in multiple deities. This drastic change was also caused by the development of several philosophies that shifted people's beliefs from many pagan cults to one single deity. Monotheism was growing in the empire even before Christianity, mainly due to Mithraism (the worship of Mithras), which was spread by Constantine's father, as well as Constantine himself. This paved the way for the Christian cult that was steadily growing during Constantine's rule.

Christians were a minority in the Roman Empire; however, they were a minority that had significant influence because they were well-organized. In fact, the Roman emperors and senators were frequently worried about the Christians because they were so well-organized in groups. The Christian organizations were first loyal to themselves and to the bishops that led them. This meant the Roman state considered them to be disloyal to the empire, so the government initiated a series of persecutions against them.

When Constantine came to power, however, his main goal was to unify the empire, and he saw Christianity as a tool that would allow him to achieve his plans. If the entire population gathered around a single deity, the empire would flourish in unity, or so Constantine thought. He was against the persecutions, and he stated that he was shocked by them, at least according to the writers of the time. It is difficult to distinguish facts from fiction in this case because many historians and witnesses believed the Christians deserved to be punished because they misbehaved; therefore, they downplayed the persecutions in their writings. Others have done the complete opposite and have exaggerated the circumstances. In any case, Christianity seemed to persuade both sides of the population, whether they were liberal or conservative in thinking, that it was the key to a unified empire.

It is known that before his conversion, Constantine's patron god was Apollo, the ancient sun god. While on his journey to fight Maxentius in 312, Constantine took a detour to visit the shrine of Apollo. There, it is claimed that Constantine received a vision from

Apollo, and he realized that the sun god was his personal protector. Once Constantine achieved victory against Maxentius, he presented himself once again to the shrine of Apollo and brought gifts to his god. These tales of his visions cannot be confirmed or denied as they were spread by orators from the cult of Apollo.

Constantine worshiped the sun god, as Apollo was often portrayed on the coinage Constantine produced. Further evidence of this is the fact that by the year 317, the pagan gods "died out," as they stopped appearing on Roman coins; however, Apollo prevailed, as he was the sole god to still be depicted on coins, art, and architecture. This personal connection that Constantine had to Apollo would make it easy for him to transition to the belief in Jesus Christ.

Many believers at the time, Constantine included, thought Christ was their beloved sun god and that both figures were, in fact, two separate aspects of one supreme deity. Apollo and Christ didn't exclude each other in the minds of the Romans; therefore, it was fairly easy to build a bridge between paganism and Christianity. For instance, the writings of Clement of Alexandria depict Jesus Christ as riding his chariot across the stars, just like Apollo was usually depicted. Statues dedicated to Jesus have also resembled the sun god. Because of this intermingling of faiths, the pagans actually believed that the Christians were simply worshipers of the sun. In addition, the Christians met during Sundays to pray together, looking to the east toward the rising sun. This act only solidified the Romans' belief that the Christians prayed to the sun god. A century later, the birth of Jesus Christ would be celebrated on December 25th, which also coincides with the winter solstice, the birth of—you guessed it—the sun god. Therefore, we can easily see how the Roman commoners would easily make the association between Christ and Apollo.

Constantine continued to gradually implement Christianity, and he developed a habit of receiving visions and dreams about Christ and various symbols, like the cross. The ancient Romans believed at the time that dreams were a gift from the divine. Therefore, they sought to understand their meaning by discussing them with various philosophers and priests. Constantine was no different. He believed in his dreams and made those around him believe in them as well. It is not known whether this was all a clever plan to reach his political goals. However, we know about one of his visions in which he saw a cross appear in the sky. Constantine claimed the soldiers saw it as well, but there is no evidence of that. His vision, however, would soon be stamped on new coins, as he saw the cross as a symbol of the divine. He often saw Christians performing the cross sign in order to ward off demons, so he was certain that he had received a divine vision and that he was protected.

Constantine was very careful and pushed Christianity slowly to avoid angering the pagan public. Most of his army was, in fact, still pagan; therefore, he used the connection he and his people saw between the sun god and Christ in order to gradually Christianize them. Constantine also started leading prayers for his troops and instructed his officers to do the same. These prayers, however, were more about teaching them a simplified way of worship of the supreme deity. Constantine knew better than to forcefully push Christianity on them because just before him, Diocletian started persecuting the Christians inside the army. Therefore, the soldiers and officers were wary about accepting the new rules of worship, and Constantine knew that he had to ensure the loyalty of the troops and that the rest would eventually follow.

Chapter 8 – Late Rule and Death

Painting depicting Constantine's baptism
(Source:https://en.wikipedia.org/wiki/Constantine_the_Great#/media/File:Raphael_
Baptism_Constantine.jpg)

In the year 326, Constantine became aware of the rumors that his wife Fausta had an affair with his son Crispus, who was born by a woman named Minervina. It is unclear whether these rumors were true or whether Fausta herself fabricated them in the hopes that Constantine would get rid of his firstborn son, making her children the next in line to inherit the throne. No matter the truth, Constantine decided to kill both Crispus and Fausta. Crispus was poisoned in Pula, Croatia, sometime between May 15th and June 17th, 326. Empress Fausta was killed by an overheated bath. Constantine made sure to wipe their names from various inscriptions and to condemn any memory of them. Even *Vita Constantini* (*Life of Constantine*), a public speech written by Eusebius of Caesarea, contains no mention of his wife Fausta or his son Crispus. It is because of the lack of contemporary sources that we cannot be sure why they were killed. The Christian stories of those times rush to portray Constantine in a good light by saying he had to punish his closest ones for their illicit relationship, which was a great sin. However, modern historians are still trying to guess what could have been the real political motive behind the murders. Some suggest Constantine killed Crispus because Fausta wished her own children to become legitimate heirs; however, this does not explain the killing of Fausta. It is possible she had to die for her children to realize that Constantine would not shy away from eliminating anyone, no matter how dear to him, if the situation demanded it.

Constantine spent his late years in his beloved Constantinople, both as his capital and as his permanent residence. He planned on reconquering Dacia, a province once abandoned under Emperor Aurelian in 285 when the Goths overtook it. This time Constantine joined forces with the tribal confederation of Sarmatians and raised a campaign against the Goths, moving the border in Dacia along the Brazda lui Novac (Romania). After the victory over the Goths, Constantine took the title Dacicus Maximus in 336.

During the final years of his life, Constantine made extensive plans for a campaign against Persia. He wrote a letter to Persia's ruler Shapur II (r. 309-379), urging him to treat Christians well since he was taking them under his patronage. There is no evidence of the date of the letter, and we can only presume it was written after the raids on the eastern border of the Roman Empire in 335 and the Persian invasion of Armenia in 336, which had been a Christian kingdom since 301. Constantine saw these events as an attack on Christianity, and he decided to campaign against Persia by leading a crusade. Bishops were called to join the crusade, and Constantine even commissioned the construction of a tent in the shape of a church that would accompany the army and offer a sacred place for prayers wherever they might find themselves.

Constantine himself wished to be baptized in the Jordan River, where Jesus himself was baptized. In his plans, this would happen right before he crossed into Persia. However, Persia sent diplomats who entered Constantinople in the winter of 336. Their mission was to seek peace. Even though Constantine could not agree to the desired peace and turned away the diplomats, the campaign was canceled, at least for the time being. But in the spring of 337, Constantine fell ill and could not resume his plans. Feeling that he might die, Constantine finally asked for the baptism to take place.

In the Christian community, baptism takes a position of great importance. It symbolizes the rebirth into a new faith, guarantees the abolition of all committed sins up until the point of the ceremony, and promises an introduction to the kingdom of heaven. According to Saint John the Baptist, who baptized Jesus, one cannot enter the kingdom of God if they are not born of water and spirit. However, before he could be baptized, Constantine had to go through a period of catechesis, which lasted for two years according to the Christian tradition. However, due to his compromised health and his status as an emperor, Constantine was granted either a full exemption or a much shorter period of catechesis.

Today, Christians are often baptized during infancy and rarely as adults. However, in the old times, baptisms of adults were common as it was believed that after the ceremony, one should not commit any sins. Many people postponed their baptism as much as they could, but Constantine took it to the extreme. Some even believe he waited on purpose to be on his deathbed before the baptism so he would be sure that all his sins would be forgiven. However, there are many other theories that explain why Constantine kept postponing his baptism, even though he showed strong convictions in Christian values during his whole life. One such theory explains that he was an emperor over both the pagans and the Christians, and in order to please both factions, he had to stay neutral. Others say that he waited for the opportunity to fulfill his wish to be baptized in the Jordan River. And some claim that Constantine thought it was unnecessary for him to be baptized as he was an instrument of God Himself. Modern historians opt to believe he delayed his baptism due to a fear of God. Constantine believed in divine anger, and it is possible he was afraid his soul would be forever lost if he committed a sin after baptism.

Constantine chose Bishop Eusebius of Nicomedia to perform the ritual of baptism. After the ceremony, Constantine retreated to his villa at Achyrion near Nicomedia, where he died. Eusebius (the historian, not the bishop) wrote that the emperor breathed his last on what he referred to as White Sunday in the year 337 on a white couch at around midday. Constantine's body was laid in a golden coffin and covered with royal purple draperies. Then the coffin and the body were transported to Constantinople to be put on display in order to receive homage from all the members of his household and principal members of his empire. When his second son, Constantius II, arrived in the city, the final rites began. Constantine was buried in a mausoleum he had built himself called the Church of the Holy Apostles.

Constantine's Legacy

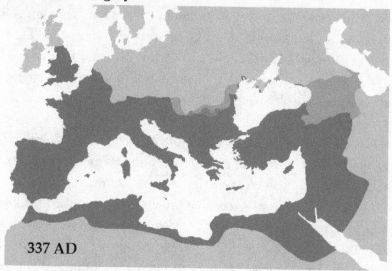

337 AD

The Roman Empire under Constantine
(Source:https://upload.wikimedia.org/wikipedia/commons/1/1c/ConstantineEmpire.
png)

In 335, Constantine the Great looked into the future and realized his empire would be in turmoil after his death. This is why he set plans in motion to divide the empire to prevent his sons from fighting each other. Constantine II was to rule over the western provinces, Constantius II would reign over the East, and Constans was set to rule Italy, Pannonia, and Africa. Constantine appointed his nephews as Caesars as well. Delmatius (also spelled as Dalmatius) ruled Thrace, Macedonia, and Achaea. His brother, Hannibalianus, was given the easternmost territories, which were detached from the main empire, and he never gained the title of king. Therefore, there were four rulers after Constantine's death: his three sons and his one nephew. What Constantine imagined was a renewed tetrarchy but with the hereditary succession system. However, Constantine couldn't foresee that another tetrarchy would fail. It was not long before the successors started plotting each other's murder. Delmatius and his brother Hannibalianus were the first to fall. Constantine II was killed in 340, and he was followed by his brother Constans ten years later. It was

Constantius II who reestablished his father's sole rule system over the whole Roman Empire. He ruled until his death in 361.

Conclusion

Constantine was the first Christian emperor, and it was he who converted the pagan Roman Empire to Christianity. It was actually the Christian historians who gave him the moniker "The Great" long after his death. Today, it is a popular opinion that he deserved such a title during his life due to his many military successes. Constantine effectively warred against the Franks (306–308 and 313–314), Alamanni (306–308), the Goths (332), and the Sarmatians (334). He also managed to return much of the Dacian province back to the Roman Empire's fold. If not interrupted by his illness, his plans against Persia would have continued and would have possibly been added to the list of his victories. Constantine is considered to be the Roman emperor who ruled the second-longest, amounting to around 31 years (Augustus holds the honor for the longest reign with an incredible 40 years).

After Constantine, ten emperors carried his name with great honor. One of them was the last emperor of the Eastern Roman Empire, Constantine XI Palaiologos. Charlemagne (742–814) often imitated Constantine the Great to show off that he was his descendant and equal. The Holy Roman Empire considered Constantine the Great to be one of the most important historical figures, as he was regarded as a warrior emperor who fought against the heathens. The Orthodox Church even elevated Constantine to the status of saint, and his celebratory day is on May 21ª. Constantine is also regarded as *isapostolos*, which means "an equal to the Apostles." He would certainly be pleased with the title, as it was recorded that he himself often said he was the thirteenth apostle. The Roman Catholic Church also regards Constantine as a saint, with the same celebration date; however, his influence is less felt in Catholicism today.

Here's another book by Captivating History
that you might be interested in

References

Cutts, E. L. (1881). *Constantine the Great: The Union of the State and the Church.* London: S.P.C.K.

Dörries, H. (1972). *Constantine the Great.* New York: Harper & Row.

Grant, M. (2009). *Constantine the Great: The Man and His Times.* New York: Barnes & Noble.

Lee, N. (2011). *Constantine the Great.* Place of publication not identified: British Library, Historic.

Smith, J. H. (1971). *Constantine the Great.* London: H. Hamilton.

CPSIA information can be obtained
at www.ICGtesting.com
Printed in the USA
LVHW030235071221
705497LV00005B/162